Eve's Wisdom

Eve's Wisdom

The Goddess Within

Illustrated by Anne Smith

Ariel Books

Andrews McMeel Publishing

Kansas City

 For information write Andrews McMeel Publishing, an Andrews McMeel Universal company, 4520 Main Street, Kansas City, Missouri 64111.

www.andrewsmcmeel.com

ISBN: 0-7407-0098-7
Library of Congress Catalog Card Number: 99-60604

Contents

Introduction 9
Elements of Eve 17
The Primal Power 65
Fulfilling Our Potential 103

Extraordinary Ordinary Women 125

Great Deeds in Myth and History 169

Suffragist Heroines 207

Words of Love 235

Meditations on the Spirit of Woman 253

Introduction

There is a potential goddess living within us all. Perhaps her presence is well-known to us; more likely, in the midst of our hectic routines of work, home, and family, we've never taken the time to meet her. Who—what—is this goddess? The very word conjures up images of the powerful spirits who were worshipped in the ancient times and who are still worshipped by some today. And so it follows that the goddess within us is a wise, strong woman. We must learn to trust her, to listen to her, to understand her.

We have had many extraordinary women grace our planet with

their presence. Some, like Joan of Arc, have made their mark on history; most are ordinary, seeking not fame or fortune but living with an intense passion and purpose to their lives. With quotations, meditations, and portraits of both uncommon and common women, this book celebrates the goddess—those women who demonstrate unusual wisdom, intelligence, self-knowledge,

confidence, and
strength—emotional,
physical, and spiritual.
We are all born with
this potential; this book
is dedicated to the
women who
cultivate it.

Elements of Eve

There have been many examples of Woman's strength in every country, at every time in history. But following are some special examples that still inspire us, urging us to improve our selves and our opportunities, and not to be afraid to be heard when what we have to say is important to the welfare of society.

Faith: Joan of Arc (1412–1431)

When she was a simple shepherd girl of sixteen, Joan of

Arc heard the voice of God telling her she had been chosen to help Him do great things. The vision urged her to help the dauphin, the oldest son of the French king, who, due to the Hundred Years'

War between France and England, was being kept from his rightful seat on the throne.

Confident of her purpose, Joan cut her hair, dressed in men's clothing, and went to see the dauphin with her offer of help. "I tell you from my Lord that you are the true heir of France and son of the king," Joan told him. Believing she was a man, he gave her four thousand troops to command. She sent a message to the English, saying, "I am a chieftain of war and whenever I meet your followers in France, I will drive them out; if they will not obey, I will put them all to death." In May 1429, Joan inspired the members of her small army to push the English out of the city of Orléans, and soon thereafter, the tide of the war turned, allowing the dauphin to be crowned King Charles VII.

In the spring of

1430, Joan was captured and sold to the English. Tried at the church court at Rouen, she was charged with witchcraft, heresy, and wearing men's clothing. The court claimed that although Joan said she heard the voice of God, she was really hearing the voice of the devil. Furthermore, they accused her of "having cast aside all womanly decency, not only to the scorn of feminine modesty, but also of wellinstructed men, she had worn the apparel and garments of most dissolute men, and in addition, had some weapons of defense." The court condemned her to death. She was burned at the stake on

May 30, 1431, at the age of nineteen. The dauphin did nothing to help her out of her grave situation.

Joan of Arc is a French heroine and symbol of nationalism as well as a universal symbol of unparalleled bravery and unshakable faith. In 1920, she was canonized by the pope and became Saint Joan.

Adaptability: La Malinche (c.1500–c.1527)

La Malinche was born a princess in the village of Viluta,

Mexico. She lived a comfortable life, receiving a good education and learning a number of languages. But when the Spanish, led by Cortés, arrived in Mexico, her life was turned upside down.

Her people offered her as a gift to the Spanish leader in the hope of stopping his conquest.

Cortés accepted La Malinche, planning to use her as an interpreter to help establish good relationships with the

Indians of Mexico. Almost overnight, La Malinche went from being a princess to a slave with no rights of her own. She kept her head, however, and made the most of her situation. In time, she came to believe that Cortés could unite the warring Indian communities, and she worked hard on his behalf. Although Cortés at first doubted her loyalty to him, she soon proved herself by alerting him to an Aztec plot to ambush him and his troops.

In 1522, La Malinche had a son by Cortés, beginning the ethnic group of people called "mestizos." Of mixed Spanish and

Indian blood, this group populates most of Mexico today.

Uprooted from her life of privilege and sold into slavery, La Malinche showed a unique ability to adapt to her new circumstances. As the symbolic mother of all mestizos, the memory of La Malinche is immortalized for future generations of Mexicans.

Dedication: Margaret Sanger (1879–1966)

Throughout her life, Margaret Sanger had a passionate interest in the issue of birth control. Perhaps because she was one of eleven children born to a mother who died at the age of fifty, she was determined to find a means of providing the poor women of New

York City and beyond with contraceptives—this during a time when only the rich could afford to buy them.

She believed vehemently that "No woman can call herself free who does not own and control her body. No woman can call herself free until she can choose consciously whether she will or will not be a mother."

Her work on behalf of women was extremely productive. She

founded Brooklyn's first birth control clinic, organized what would later be known as the Planned Parenthood Federation of America, and toured throughout the world in support of making birth control available to women everywhere.

Sanger did not choose a popular field of work. She met disapproval on every front from a public that was not ready for her, and endured indictment and arrest. She also suffered great personal loss in the death of her five-year-old daughter and divorce from her husband. But still she continued, for more than fifty years, to fight for the reproductive rights of all women, the benefits of which we all enjoy today.

Strength: Frida Kahlo (1907–1954)

While she was a teenager, Frida Kahlo suffered a terrible accident that would leave her semi-crippled for the rest of her life. During her recuperation she took up painting, and thus began to create a body of work that would become a treasure within Mexico and throughout the world.

Her art, known for its primitive style and bright colors, was intensely personal. Physical pain, emotional disappointment, sorrow for her inability to have children—all were depicted in her paintings. After her death, the Mexican government, in order to ensure that her paintings never left the country permanently, declared them national treasures.

The circumstances of Kahlo's life might easily have destroyed a weaker spirit. She endured chronic pain, suffered from three miscarriages, had a rocky and unfaithful relationship with her famous husband, the painter Diego Rivera, and was often overshadowed by his fame. Yet she continued to paint with passion and energy, demonstrating the incredible strength that could not be held down by a weakened body.

Loyalty: Ruth

Perhaps the person best remembered for her loyalty is Ruth,

the Moabitess of the Old Testament. The story begins when Naomi, her husband, and their two sons leave Bethlehem to live in Moab. Naomi's two sons marry two Moab women—Ruth and Orpah.

Some time later, Naomi's husband dies, and ten years later, her two sons die also, leaving the three women alone. Naomi, wanting to return to Bethlehem, urges her daughters-in-law to remain in Moab with their mothers' families, to find new husbands and be happy.

Orpah agrees to stay behind, but Ruth does not. Instead, she utters these famous words: "Do not urge me to leave you or turn back from following you; for where you go, I will go, and where you lodge, I will lodge. Your people shall be my people, and your God, my god. Where you die, I will die, and there I will be buried. Thus may the

Lord do to me, and worse, if anything but death parts you and me."

Bravery: Boudicca (First Century BC)

This British queen is a strong example of womanly war power.

Her kingdom (near Norfolk/Suffolk) was brutally seized by the Romans trying to extend their empire east. Boudicca's fiery Celtic spirit refused to submit to the invaders and she raised a huge army to fight them off. She and her troops conquered at least three large Roman settlements, including Londinium, the early city of London. Boudicca, in defense of her own people, showed no mercy to the enemy and executed almost seventy thousand Roman soldiers. Taking on a role most would assume was reserved for a man, Boudicca's actions demonstrated that women are capable of enormous emotional strength and bravery.

The Primal Power

Comrades, I say to you,
Spare no effort, struggle
unceasingly,
That at last peace may
come to our people.
And jewelled dresses and
deformed feet
Will be abandoned.
And one day, all under heaven

Will see beautiful free
women,
Blooming like fields of
flowers,
And bearing brilliant
and noble
human beings.
—Qiu Jin

Women have had a prominent position in many societies in a variety of cultures throughout the world since the beginning of time. Although there is no evidence of a matriarchal society—one politically and economically controlled by women—there is plenty of support for *matrilineal* societies, where descent is traced through the mother. While the position of women in these early societies was not generally strong by today's standards, it's interesting to consider what it would have been like to live in some of these ancient cultures, when women sometimes had more rights than we might suppose.

If you had been a woman living in Babylonia around 1750 B.C., you would have been permitted a surprising degree of financial independence. Although your parents would have arranged your marriage and your husband would have had complete control over the marriage and the children, your dowry would have remained your own. After your death, your property would go not to your husband, but directly to your children.

Ancient Egyptian society was male dominated, but women enjoyed some important rights in law and business. As a woman during those times, you would have been able to dispose of your private property in any way you chose. You could also lend money to your husband and charge interest! And though the tradition was not always adhered to, the right to the Egyptian throne was supposed to have been passed through the female line.

Women played a significant role in the society of Minoan Crete. Religion appears to have been goddess-based: Here you might have served as a priest or an administrator. Should you have been so inclined, you could have participated equally with men in sports and games such as boxing and bull-jumping—grasping the bull's horns and vaulting over its back.

Consider the respect given to some of the women in Jewish liturgy. There was Sarah, mother of Isaac; Rebekah, mother of Esau and Jacob; Rachel, mother of Joseph and Benjamin; and Leah, mother of Levi, Simeon, Reuben, Judah, Issachar, and Zebulon. In times of trouble, these "matriarchs" were called upon as a source of spiritual help, and in fact, the Exodus from Egypt was viewed as a reward for their dedication to God. They also held the status of prophets. In the eyes of some scholars, the matriarchs were partners in the development of Judaism.

It would not have been at all difficult to protect your rights if you had lived in ancient Ireland and Wales, where Celtic law was highly favorable to women. It was a land of equal pay for equal work, so you would have been paid for doing housework! You would also have been well protected from violence inside and outside of marriage. The opportunity was there for you to govern and engage in politics or religious life. You could be a law-giver, you could own private property separate from marriage, and you could even decide whom you wanted to marry and when. Laws existed that protected against sexual harassment. In this ancient society, women were honored as much for their minds as for their bodies, and even went to war.

Women in Sparta not only owned two-thirds of the land, they also had the option of becoming warriors. But in more cultured Athens, equality wasn't the case at all. You would have been prohibited from making any significant business exchanges, and you would not be allowed to participate in the courts. You would not even be permitted to attend performances in Greek theater, where men assumed the female roles.

But you had your moment when it came time for the *Thesmophoria*, an exclusively female celebration held each year in Greece. This three-day festival involved secret ceremonies honoring Demeter, the goddess of agriculture and marriage. These rites of passage were thought to assure fertility. Women so strictly controlled the rite that men feared physical harm for any intrusion.

If you had lived in ancient Rome, you would have most definitely been in a male-dominated society. Yet it appears that a few women became gladiators! These may have originally been war hostages or criminals, but all types of women could become involved in the games, and by the first century A.D., many noblewomen had taken up the sword. Their battles, though fought to the death, were billed as novelties, much like today's boxing matches featuring women.

If you had lived on the other side of the Atlantic as a female member of the Paiute or Shoshone American Indian tribes, you would have carried the chief economic burden for your people. You

were responsible not only for bearing and raising your children, but you were also the principal gatherer and provider of food. You might have been known for your weaving and shamanism, and if you were powerful enough, you could take on more than one husband.

In the Iroquois tribe, lineage was *matrilineal*, which meant that a child inherited his or her identity as well as personal property through the mother's line. As an Iroquois woman, you would have lived together with your whole family, or clan, in one dwelling. The oldest woman, known as the "mother," presided over the clan, and had the right to nominate chiefs. Aside from the most personal possessions, like clothing and weapons, everything belonged to the women.

When you married, your husband would leave his home to come to yours. Since the men spent most of the time hunting, your husband would be away much of the time. This left you and the other women to take care of planting and harvesting, as well as managing hearth and home. In fact, you did it all!

Fulfilling Our Potential

For today's women, there are so many ways in which we can use our skills and energies to attain feelings of success and achievement—raising our children, excelling in our chosen careers, volunteering in our communities, and keeping our relationships with others alive, vibrant, and meaningful.

I do not want to die . . . until I have faithfully made the most of my talent and cultivated the seed that was placed in me until the last small twig has grown.

—Käthe Kollwitz

People are not the best because they work hard. They work hard because they are the best.

—Bette Midler

You don't have to have a title or a position to be effective.

—Wilma Mankiller

Growth itself contains the germ of happiness.

—Pearl S. Buck

No one can arrive from being talented alone. God gives talent, work transforms talent into genius.

—Anna Pavlova

What I have done in my life I have done because I wanted to do it and because it interested me. I just happen to be a woman, and I don't believe it has made much difference.

—Mary Leakey

To love what you do and feel that it matters—how could anything be more fun?

—Katharine Graham

Human beings are not so constituted that they can live without expansion. If they do not get it one way, they must another, or perish.

—Margaret Fuller

I was taught that the way of progress is neither swift nor easy.

—Marie Curie

There's a period of life when we swallow a knowledge of ourselves, and it becomes either good or sour inside.

—Pearl Bailey

Once I decide to do something, I can't have people telling me I can't. If there's a roadblock, you jump over it, walk around it, crawl under it.

—Kitty Kelley

Neither woman nor man lives by work, or love, alone. . . . The human self defines itself and grows through love and *work: All psychology before and after Freud boils down to that.*

—Betty Friedan

I loved the feeling of freedom in running, the fresh air, the feeling that the only person I'm really competing with is me.

—Wilma Rudolph

It's a sad day when you find out that it's not accident or time or fortune but just yourself that kept things from you.

—Lillian Hellman

It is never too late to be what you might have been.

—George Eliot

Extraordinary
Ordinary
Women

Sometimes, all it takes to effect a change is a strong will and determination. These "ordinary" extra-

ordinary women have proven that you don't have to be rich or famous to make your indelible mark on the world.

Clara Hale

Beginning in 1940, Clara Hale became a foster mother to more than forty children of all races, creeds, and colors. Then, as drug abuse problems all but overran her Harlem, New York, community, she really went into action. Within a mere six months, she housed twenty-two babies of heroin-addicted mothers in her modest, five-room apartment. It wasn't long before she helped establish the first home for infants who were born drug addicted. Before her death in 1993, Clara "Mother" Hale had cared for more than five hundred children at Hale House, founded in 1975. Hale House was known as the Center for the Promotion of Human Potential. At that time, it was the only black voluntary agency in the United States.

Sang Lan

Despite the terrible adversity of suffering a spinal injury that paralyzed her from the waist down during the 1998 Goodwill Games, this seventeen-year-old

Chinese gymnast's positive attitude and glowing spirit are a true inspiration. Since her accident, she has become something of an international symbol of what courage and happiness can do. She has shown great perseverance in rehabilitating herself and gaining strength, but more important, she always has a smile on her face.

Christa McAuliffe

From the classroom to the annals of history, Christa McAuliffe has left her mark. In 1986, this extraordinary ordinary woman was to have been the first civilian in space. Unfortunately, the NASA mission ended tragically: Only seventy-three seconds after liftoff, the *Challenger* space shuttle exploded, killing all seven astronauts on board.

Picked out of

11,500 applicants, Christa was chosen mainly because, although she was a gifted teacher, she was an ordinary person. Her presence helped boost the profile of the space program and generated new interest among the public. Christa, as a teacher and through her participation in the space program, wanted to inspire future generations to accomplish anything they set out to do.

Carolyn McCarthy

When this Long Island woman—wife, mother, nurse—suffered great loss and tragedy at the hands of a mad gunman in the Long Island Rail-road massacre, she set out to make a difference. Her husband was killed and her son severely wounded on that fateful evening, and she was incredulous that her local representative would not vote in favor of stricter gun control laws in her district. Outraged, she herself ran for congressional office, and despite all the odds, came out a winner. Congresswoman McCarthy won her second term in the 1998 elections.

Oseola McCarty

In July 1995, this eighty-seven-year-old laundress surprised everyone when she donated her life savings of $150,000 to the University of Southern

Mississippi in order to establish a scholarship fund for deserving and needy young people, especially African-Americans. Her unselfishness was particularly touching since she herself had been unable to attend college. Oseola left school in the sixth grade to care for a sick aunt. She had done other people's washing and ironing for more than seventy-five years. A natural-born saver, the few dollars she'd bring in accumulated over the years. She never married and felt that she wanted the money to go the college. Although she expressed some regret that she couldn't do everything or that she could do more, she knew she could do something to help somebody. And she did.

Florence Nightingale

The quintessential nurse extraordinaire, this name has become synonymous with unselfish nurturing and care. When she was a young woman living in England, Nightingale left her rich, upper-class family to train as a nurse, and soon became a hospital administrator. During the Crimean War in the 1850s, she showed her administrative genius by organizing a hospital unit of thirty-eight nurses. Among her many contributions, she enforced a code of discipline, introduced much-needed sanitary regulations, and set up a system for securing the necessary supplies. Known as the "Lady of the Lamp," she would often walk through the wards at night carrying a lamp, encouraging and comforting the patients under her care.

Dorothy Eustis

A longtime breeder of German shepherds, in 1930 Dorothy Eustis established a school to train dogs as guides for the blind. Born in Philadelphia, Eustis moved to Switzerland as an adult, where she raised a special class of German shepherds that were trained for military and police work. These dogs were particularly intelligent, alert, and responsive, and

Eustis began to wonder what other functions such dogs might fill.

In 1923, Eustis visited a school she had heard about in Potsdam, Germany, where dogs were being trained as guides for war veterans who had lost their sight. Later, when she re-turned to the United States, she organized The Seeing Eye in Morristown, New Jersey, a training school for guide dogs for the blind that still exists today.

By the time of Eustis's death in 1946, the school had trained more than 1,300 dogs.

Rosa Parks

Perhaps one of the best-known symbols of the civil rights movement, Rosa Parks, a black woman, did the unheard-of—she refused to give up her seat on a bus to a white man in 1955. This seamstress and housekeeper was arrested for violating the segregation laws of Montgomery, Alabama. The incident sparked a 382-day mass boycott of the Montgomery bus system, which eventually led to the desegregation of the city's buses. Rosa Park's action was one of the precipitating events of the civil rights movement.

Estelle Sapir

At seventy-one years old, this Holocaust survivor and daughter of a Nazi victim (a Warsaw banker killed in Majdanek) successfully became the first person to receive a settlement in the United States of a Holocaust-era claim against a Swiss bank. Credit Suisse is one of the banks involved in class-action lawsuits to reclaim assets hoarded from Jewish victims.

Ms. Sapir, a diminutive woman, has had a strong voice and a strong presence in seeing this story to its just conclusion.

Jody Williams

Founding coordinator of the International Campaign to Ban Landmines (ICBL), which was launched in 1992, Jody Williams has written and spoken extensively on the problem of land mines and the need to ban them. Emphasizing the horrors that result from land mine explosions, especially to children and other civilians, she has served as the chief strategist and spokesperson for the campaign. Ms. Williams was awarded the Nobel Peace Prize in 1997 for her work on this worthy cause. Prior to her affiliation with the ICBL, she developed and directed humanitarian

relief projects and was
a teacher of English as
a second language in

Washington, D.C., the United Kingdom, and Mexico.

Great Deeds in Myth and History

The reason for Lady Godiva's famous ride through the streets of Coventry, England, was that her husband had imposed taxes that his wife and the townspeople thought were too heavy. Her husband agreed to lift the taxes only if Lady Godiva would ride naked on horseback through the town—which she did.

The most successful conductor on the Underground Railroad, which transported slaves to freedom in the North, was Harriet Tubman, an illiterate former slave.

The six Vestal Virgins of ancient Rome were the most sacred mortal women in that city. Their job was to keep the sacred fire of Vesta's hearth burning—the fire that symbolized the heart of the

Roman Empire. Chosen at an early age from patrician families, the Vestal Virgins served for thirty years.

The first woman lawyer to argue a case before the Supreme

Court was Belva Ann Lockwood, in 1879.

During the Revolutionary War, a woman named Deborah Sampson dressed as a man and served for a year and a half at West Point, until her secret was discovered by a doctor after she was wounded in battle.

Mary Cassatt, one of the great Impressionist painters,

did much of her early work abroad, where she gained wide recognition for her work—despite her sex. Her visit home was reported in a Philadelphia newspaper as the arrival of "Mary Cassatt, sister of Mr.

Cassatt, President of the Pennsylvania Railroad, who has been studying painting in France and owns the smallest Pekingese dog in the world."

The Amazons of classical mythology were warrior women of commanding size and great skill in battle. They were supposed to have burned off their right breasts so that they would be able to wield a bow and arrow more easily.

When Amelia Earhart guided her Lockheed Vega on the 2,026-mile flight from Newfoundland to Ireland, she became the first woman to fly solo across the Atlantic. This much-heralded accomplishment put her in the public spotlight until 1937, when her plane was lost at sea and she was presumed dead. Earhart's legacy was clear in a letter she left behind: "Women must try to do things as men have tried. When they fail, their failure must be but a challenge to others."

Sojourner Truth, born a slave under

the name of Isabella Baumfree, traveled throughout the country in the 1800s speaking out against slavery. Setting out with only a quarter and a new dress, she stopped at church meetings and street corners to preach her message. Tall and gaunt, she is said to have had a deep, powerful voice and the air of a queen. Later, she took up the cause of women's rights and made her famous "Ain't

I a Woman" speech.

In 1872, Victoria Claflin Woodhull announced her candidacy for the U.S. presidency on the People's Party ticket. Her running mate was to be freedman Frederick Douglass. Despite much hard work, she was unable to get on the ballot.

Penelope, wife of Odysseus, was beset by suitors during her husband's long absence.

Under tremendous pressure to choose one of the suitors to replace Odysseus, whom everyone but Penelope considered long dead, Penelope used her wits to figure out a way of putting the decision off.

She promised to choose once she had finished weaving her father's shroud, but each night she undid the weaving she had done during the day, and thus held out until Odysseus came home again.

When Sandra Day O'Connor became the first woman to serve on the Supreme Court in 1981, she acknowledged the long struggle women had undergone for equal rights in the United States by saying, "I happily share that honor with millions of American women of yesterday and today."

At a time when women had little education and power, Queen Elizabeth I ruled England with a steady hand, bringing forty-five years of great prosperity to the country, and creating an environment in which the arts flourished.

Pearl S. Buck wrote more than a hundred books, many of which are about life in China, where she lived for much of her life.

When she won the Nobel Prize for Literature in 1935, she was the first woman to do so.

Frances Perkins, secretary of labor under President

Franklin Roosevelt, was the first female cabinet member in American history.

During the seventh century B.C., Sappho wrote poetry about love and relationships that was so admired by Plato, he called her the "tenth Muse."

Barbara Jordan, who had to ride in the "colored" section of the local bus as a young girl, in 1966 became the first woman ever to serve in the Texas State Senate. Soon gaining recognition for her powerful oratory and her concern for America's poor and downtrodden, she was elected to the U.S. House of Representatives, where she served six years until her retirement in 1978.

Montessori schools are based on the ideas of Maria Montessori, an Italian educator of the twentieth century. She believed that children learn best through their own desire to accomplish and create. Montessori education, now widespread, is most often used at the preschool and kindergarten levels.

When Meriwether Lewis and William Clark made their historic trip of exploration into the Pacific Northwest, they were guided by a fur trapper and his Shoshoni wife, Sacajawea. For eight thousand miles, Sacajawea served as guide and interpreter. She smoothed the way through the Indian lands, obtained horses to cross the mountains, and when supplies ran low one winter, showed the explorers which roots could be safely eaten, probably saving the men from starvation.

Mary Lyon didn't have the money to go to the school she wanted to attend, so she wove two blankets and offered them as tuition. Her offer was accepted, and in 1817, Lyon enrolled at the Sanderson

Academy in Ashfield, Massachusetts. Twenty years later, Mary founded Mount Holyoke Female Seminary in South Hadley, Massachusetts, one of the first all-female colleges in the United States.

Suffragist Heroines

We ask justice, we ask equality, we ask that all civil and political rights that belong to citizens of the United States, be guaranteed to us and our daughters forever." These words were spoken by Elizabeth Cady Stanton at a time when American women had few legal rights and no say whatsoever in the government. It took decades of hard work before Stanton's dreams were realized—hard work and amazing courage demonstrated by thousands of women throughout the country who refused to accept the position of second-class citizens. These women took a good look at their situation, listened to the goddess within, and took action.

The first known demand for suffrage in the United States was made in 1647 by Margaret Brent of Maryland, but it wasn't until the mid-1800s that the movement really got under way. One of the catalysts was the Civil War, which thrust women into new roles in both the South and the North, giving them new skills and greater confidence. While the men were busy fighting, women had run farms and businesses, worked as nurses, spies—even soldiers—and filled factory and office positions. After the war was over, it was difficult for many to go back to the status quo, and the women's suffrage movement gained momentum. In 1866, suffragists presented Congress with petitions bearing ten thousand signatures asking for the vote—a petition that was largely ignored.

In 1869, the National Woman Suffrage Association (later the National American Woman Suffrage Association), spearheaded by Stanton and Susan B. Anthony, was formed with the goal of securing women the right to vote through an amendment to the Constitution. Stanton, a brilliant speaker and writer, furnished the ideas while Anthony handled the organization.

During the 1872 election, Victoria Woodhull proclaimed that the Fourteenth Amendment, which was ratified in 1868 and which makes no mention of gender, actually enfranchised women. So encouraged, hundreds of women went to the polls all over the country demanding to vote in the presidential election, but they were turned away. Some were actually arrested for attempting to vote.

American suffragists came from all walks of life. Working-class women in the cities, who found themselves working long hours in appalling conditions for very little pay, were among the first to join the movement. As they began to strike and form picket lines, they found support from women in the middle and upper classes. As Anthony stated, "There will never be complete equality until women themselves help to make laws and elect lawmakers." When extremely wealthy women joined the suffragists, they were able to finance political campaigns that gave the movement new power.

By 1910, suffrage was known by a new name, "Votes for Women." Frustrated by the obstacles they faced, the suffragists were growing bolder and more aggressive, moving out of their parlors into the streets, where they staged marches, argued before groups of working-class men, and pressured politicians. The violence surrounding their agitations grew, and they were sometimes arrested, fined, and imprisoned.

Carrie Chapman Catt and Alice Paul joined the fray during this period. Paul, who had taken part in the extremely militant suffragist movement in Britain, pushed for more radical measures. As a result, she and many others were arrested and imprisoned. When they went on hunger strikes to protest their imprisonment, they were force-fed like so many of their sisters in England. This treatment provoked more protests, which in turn led to more arrests.

When the United States entered World War I in 1917, once again war brought women unparalleled opportunities. They took on jobs and responsibilities that put them miles ahead in terms of experience and confidence. Women volunteered overseas as nurses and ambulance drivers, worked in manufacturing plants, drove streetcars, took over stores and businesses—in short, took on more responsibility than ever before. The skills and experience they gained brought them new confidence.

And finally, the tide began to turn on women's right to vote. Several states adopted women's suffrage in 1918. President Wilson publicly supported the federal women's suffrage amendment that same year. Although neither Anthony nor Stanton survived to see it, on August 26, 1920, the Nineteenth Amendment, guaranteeing women the right to vote, was ratified. It stated: "The Right of

citizens of the
United States to
vote shall not be
denied or abridged
by the United

States or by any State
on account of sex."
Close to twenty-six
million women now
had the right to vote.

Words
of Love

The need to give and receive love in a woman's life is a major driving force in who we become and what has meaning for each of us. But understanding love and its responsibilities is no easy education.

Many great women have offered their thoughts and experiences on this most important subject.

The giving of love is an education in itself.

—Eleanor Roosevelt

Nothing in life is as good as the marriage of true minds between man and woman.

—Pearl S. Buck

The best marriages, like the best lives, were both happy and unhappy. There was even a kind of necessary tension, a certain tautness between the partners that gave the

marriage strength, like the tautness of a full sail. You went forward on it.

—Anne Morrow Lindbergh

What we have once enjoyed we can never lose. All that we love deeply becomes a part of us.

—Helen Keller

Marriage, to women as to men, must be a luxury, not a necessity; an incident of life, not all of it.

—Susan B. Anthony

No partner in a love relationship . . . should feel that he has to give up an essential part of him-self to make it viable.

—May Sarton

Love is like quicksilver in the hand. Leave the fingers open, and it stays. Clutch it, and it darts away.

—Dorothy Parker

Love is a fire. But whether it is going to warm your hearth or burn down your house, you can never tell.

—Joan Crawford

All these reverend gentlemen who insist on the word "obey" in the marriage service should be removed for a clear violation of the Thirteenth Amendment to the Federal Constitution, which says there shall be neither slavery nor involuntary servitude within the United States.

—Elizabeth Cady Stanton

I like not only to be loved, but to be told I am loved.

—George Eliot

Only love can be divided endlessly and still not diminish.

—Anne Morrow Lindbergh

But surely for everything you love you have to pay some price.

—Agatha Christie

Meditations on the Spirit of Woman
by K. Testa

A woman's thoughts are like ancient grains of sand; they construct pyramids of erudition.

When the thirst for guidance parches the lips, a woman's well of wisdom infinitely satiates.

Prudence and knowledge walk hand in hand, but Woman guides them into wisdom's domain.

A woman's wisdom is like an intoxicating libation.

Darkness bade farewell as the dawn enlightened the earth; such is a woman's role in bringing about understanding.

There is alchemy in a woman's intellect; she transforms our base thoughts into golden dreams.

The intellectual strength of a woman opens the doors of perception.

Her crystal ship sails us into the realm of omniscience.

*The woman who is
Athenian of mind
infuses consciousness with
arrows of wisdom.*

Women of inner strength are the high priestesses of society.

The cerebral woman plays Jesus to the Lazarus in our souls.

A girl accepts knowledge; a woman dissects it, uses it.

A woman of strength is a sorceress who conjures up potions of possibility.

These protectors of the Seasons, these guardians of the grain, these powerful threats to man's intellect, these are women of witch-craft.

Woman of vision,
stain the eyes
of time.

The Maid of Orléans lives eternal in the hearts of steadfast women.

When women present the emeralds of their mind, a wealth of wisdom enriches us all.

The Song of Deborah celebrates the woman of vision.

Book design, art direction,
and composition by
Diane Hobbing of
Snap-Haus Graphics
in Edgewater, NJ